That Other Side of My Brain

That Other Side of My Brain

Mike Varga

Copyright © 2018 by Mike Varga

All rights reserved. No part of this book may be reproduced or transmitted in any form or by any means without written permission from the author.

Editing & Layout: Writer Services, LLC
Cover Design: Lori Varga Smith

ISBN 10: 1-942389-16-7
ISBN 13: 978-1-942389-16-3

Prominent Books and the Prominent Books Logo are Trademarks of Prominent Books, LLC

Contents

Prologue: That Other Side of My Brain ix

Part 1: Just for Fun 1
    Pen and Paper 3
    Sunbeam 4
    The Little Boy in Me 5
    The Old Man and Me 6
    Roller Coaster 7
    Much the Way I like It 8
    Sunflower Summer 9
    Winter's Bite 10
    El Niño Florida 11
    Writer's Block 12
    Our Friend the Moon 12
    Alone Connecting with Me 13
    Restlessness 14
    Spring is in the Air 15
    A Summer's Day 16
    Adventures Sail 17
    Sailing Along With Me 18
    Riding High 19

Dreams 20

Mother Earth 21

Another Night on the Road 22

Dropping in on Morning Rush Hour 23

Football at Midnight 24

Scotch and Me 25

A Little More 26

Shhh! 27

Symmetry in Five-Word Lines 28

If I Could Dream on Cue 29

Water and You 30

A Field of Black and White 31

Maybe Tomorrow I will 32

Christmas Throughout the Year 33

I'm the Dude in 9C 34

Feet up at the End of the Day 35

What is That Dollar Worth? 35

It Must be Here 36

My Friend the Trees 37

Just a Boat Tied by the Sea 38

Fall's Coming! 39

Musician's Passion 40

Karaoke 41

Part 2: The World as I See It 43

Migration 44

When Night Becomes Most Dark 45

Life's Lottery 46

Migraine 48

Fever's Hold on Me	50
So, You Want my Vote	51
Mountain Reckoning	52
Tears for Aleppo	53
What a Waste	55
An Accident at Rush Hour	56
Pick-up Baseball	57
Beneath a Scarlet Sky	59
In Honor of Miosotis Familia	61
Patriot's Ideals	62
No Chance	63
Workers' Struggle	64
Body, Mind and Soul	64
I Had a Friend	66

Part 3: Philosophy and Me 67

Sincerely	69
Wisdom	70
What do you Believe?	71
Both of Me	72
Building of Logic	73
Rounded	74
This Poem Writes Itself	75
Changes	76
Of Love, Wisdom and Truth	77
The Other Side	81
Unlocking the Door	82
Whispers on the Wind	83
Keep Her Close	84

Dancing with Circumstance 85
Listen and Learn 86
When You Were Eleven. 87
Elusiveness of Tranquility. 88
My Forest. 89
Loving Curiosity 90
Thinking About It 91
Keep it Simple … Some Thoughts.… 91
Of Perspective and Shading 92
The Burden. 94
In the Smallness of Time 95
Time Traveled 96
Off to School. 97
By the Long Island Sound 100
The Next Day .101
Embracing Risks. 102
Passion 104
Passion is a Dragon 106
Be Lucky 107

About the Author 111

Prologue:
That Other Side of My Brain

I have been for a long time engaged in the business of business and the application of engineering, math, logic, and science, along with the art of psychology. The psychology was always geared to get people to follow, or to develop them into effective leaders, to build a brand, even a persona that becomes the vessel of one's reputation. Reputation of course is built through layers of success, through painful-at-times deployment of integrity, and, above all, persistence. Persistence borne out of passion and an ability to abstract myself from situations to gain useful and truthful perspective were my strengths. Persistence, perspective, and curiosity were my friends in a journey through my business career.

I have, as of late, found that passion, perspective and curiosity have found their way into my journey as a writer.

There is an underlying cold logic in the psychology of business that I've applied over the years. It begins with a philosophy I had to execute relentlessly to achieve the long-term objectives. That philosophy included an honest appraisal of my strengths and weaknesses and the reality of situations—what I could control and could not, what I was capable of and what I was not. I felt that I must never fool myself. If I did, then there are no possible tools that could be used to improve, no way to succeed, and no way to deliver against my own expectations. Writing poetry and exposing myself in thought and soul is a natural extension of that philosophy with a creative twist. I like the use of rhythm and rhyme as a way to convey passion and enhance the feeling of words and to explore words and ideas with relentless curiosity. I've striven to deliver ideas creatively in the works I present herein.

Certainly, there is creativity in the "art" of business. However, unless you really look for the nuances in business, you may miss the artistry. So here I use the right side of my brain, with a small dose of left side of my brain, to arrive at this compilation of poems. It took me a couple years to develop this content, and in that time I found my style changed some. These works are not organized chronologically, resulting in a mix of styles as you read.

I have thought much about exposing my soul and my thoughts through these works, but I find that these are at best only still a glimpse of who I am. This may be more meaningful to me in the context of my life than other accomplishments, but quite possibly not in the eyes of others. I'm sure I can never fully succeed in exposing my soul and my mind as I had attempted. There's always something that holds me back a little. Maybe it's dark places or thoughts that should never find the light of day. Or maybe it's simply ego that keeps one from fully exploring and exposing weaknesses or scars and vulnerabilities.

When I first started writing, I didn't really share very much with others. I had fear of criticism as well as exposure. At the same time, I really knew that to be true to my personal philosophy, I needed to be brave. I did learn from my business experience that only through risk-taking, lesson-learning and the sting of criticism can we really grow.

Of course, a more worrisome outcome of my writing is that no one would really even notice. Ironic, to worry about exposing my soul and talent or lack thereof while at the same time realizing that few might actually read these works. In the first few poems I printed, I put the following lines on the first page to express this sentiment:

> *Check my ego at the lion's lair*
> *Exposing my soul without a care*
> *Little will the world later note*
> *What this writer here hath wrote*

I've written poetry about myself, about the world around me, the interaction between people, and then sometimes I wrote rhymes and thoughts just for the plain fun of it. I found when looking at my poems that most of them made me feel something when I wrote them, and still make me feel something when I read them, and I hope that you, the reader, find meaning and maybe feel something too. I choose poetry as an expression of thought because I have always admired those who can say something very meaningful in few words and do it in a way that entertains the senses as well as the mind.

I have tried to organize these works in some logical order. That's the right side of my brain working here again. Then I changed my mind. Sometimes, I'll tie things together that have a meaning I would like to impart, and sometimes I'll just play out some fun poems. After all, this is about using the other side of my brain! "Part 1" is comprised of fun poems; they have some meaning but are mostly just playing with words and thoughts about experiences and trying out rhythm and rhymes. "Part 2" is the world as I see it. The poems in this part of the book are my attempt to express the challenges and experiences of being human in this world today. Here, I am trying to say something that's important, good or bad, touching or sad. Lastly, "Part 3" has poems that are most important to me. They are poems about philosophy and myself—an attempt to express who I am and what I believe.

Many times, I'm asked, "What does a poem mean?" I usually answer with a question: "What does it mean to you?" The point of the question is not to be flippant about poetry. In fact, I'm really quite serious about poetry and about poetry having meaning, sometimes layered meaning. Is it really about something as simple as changing seasons, or is it a metaphor for an aging process? I wish to make people *feel* as well as think about messages. It's quite possible that some readers may surmise meaning and gain understanding that I didn't know was there, at least at a conscious level. I know there are times when my subconscious plays a role in the words and rhyme of a poem. Occasionally in this book, I will provide some explanation or lead-in but without the intent of providing a full description of what I was thinking or feeling when I wrote the poem. I really hope the reader rather enjoys discovering that for themselves. Besides, a little mystery is always fun.

Part 1:
Just for Fun

I've written about numerous things that have little to no meaning or depth, sometimes it's just plain fun. Sometimes, fun is writing in pen and paper and seeing the number of mistakes and how a poem evolves, and sometimes it's an attempt at symmetry in five-word lines. You may find some meaning creeping in fun poems, but it was most likely entirely inadvertent. But you never know, so watch for it!

Pen and Paper

A heavy pen and paper white
Thoughtfully compose and make it right
~~Liky~~ Like poets of ancient times
Working out thoughts and careful rhymes
Mistakes you could readily ~~so~~ find
Or hesitance and change of mind
The flow of ink across the pages
Captured thought and texture for the ages
The beauty of being outside while to write
Birds of prey wheel in flight
Ospreys hunting for their meal
Like searching for words to make us feel
More often failing and trying again
So crossed out and try again
Discipline of mind and thought
Perfect words and phrases sought
Overcoming this minds of utility
~~Paper a~~ Pen and Paper's the ~~purest~~ utility

Mite

Pen and Paper

A heavy pen and paper white
Thoughtfully compose and make it right
Like poets of ancient times

Working out thoughts and careful rhymes
Mistakes you could readily find
Or hesitance and change of mind

The flow of ink across the pages
Captured thought and texture for the ages
The beauty of being outside while I write

Birds of prey wheel in flight
Ospreys hunting for their meal
Like search for words to make us feel

More often failing and trying again
So cross it out and try again
Discipline of mind and thought

Perfect words and phrases sought
Overcoming this mind's futility
Pen and paper's the perfect utility

Sunbeam

Still and lazy awaiting the day
Calm and rested for now
Life's worries and hustle at stay

Sunbeam sneaks into the room
Something new to observe
Particles alighted from the gloom

Supported on a cushion of air
Propelled and set in motion
By what passion and such flair

Left and Right or Up and Down
Do they care where they go?
Intents only my mind has sown

At such times I observe
Other thoughts would invade
Such luxuries do I deserve?

Words describe feeling
Or what I really see
Thoughts and ideas yielding

Sunbeam brighten my day
Slowly moving across the room
And hasten me on my way

The Little Boy in Me

This poem is about staying connected to that little boy inside me, as is obvious by the title. I have often blamed the mischievousness I have within me on a little boy inside me. I wrote this poem while in my mother's house one quiet morning while waiting for everyone else to wake. I was enjoying the thought that just maybe for Mom, I was still a little boy.

The Little Boy in Me

Hold me on your knee
Play with me in your mind
The little boy inside of me

Teach me of sun and moon
Roll with me rock and stone
Sing to me a pretty tune

I want to be your little boy
I promise I will be good
Give me some time and toy

Protect me and hold my hand
I am but a little boy and unsure
Help me walk today in the sand

By the ocean of white and blue
Walk with me, splash and play
Young, pretty we are all new

Now for the other side of that "little boy"....

The Old Man and Me

I look in the mirror and see gray
I feel as if I'm twenty if I'm but a day

My mind says I'm a boy in baseball hat
But my stomach is clearly no longer flat

It looks easy, muscles twitch to play
But when mind says go, they just stay

Pretty young ladies, I notice and still see
But if they notice, it's an old man that's me

In my mind I can still work hard and long
But experience is smart and seldom wrong

Must be better to age, keeping heart young
Then to not and hear that final bell rung

Maybe I'll learn to age gracefully
Or not and continue as me playfully

This, I guess, is but a little rhyme
Something old men do to pass the time

Roller Coaster

My body reluctant pushed high
See in front of me the cloudy sky

Pitched forward like a rock off a cliff
Falling faster, smooth breeze, scared stiff

Involuntary screams escape each of us
The thrill of journeys high within us

More ups and faster downs
New twists and even faster turns

Thrills and jostles
Struggle and wrestles

Up, down, and around to where we started
Wobbly, stomach uncertain with this ride we've departed

The line is short
Shall we go again?

Much the Way I like It

The morning is quiet and still much the way I like it
Light shimmers on the pond reflections clearly rippled

Alone in thoughts, emotions and hope
Quietly I write to no one and to know just one

Birds play, a blackbird crows and yet it seems quiet
Plane disrupts nature with high flight overhead

I feel everything and yet nothing at all
Why do I write these thoughts that are nothing at all

I read a poem about azaleas this morning in the paper
It was nice, but I imagine it was some musings like mine

No words of importance, no rhythm and rhyme
But random thoughts, much the way I like it

Sunflower Summer

*Sunflower bright and beautiful in field today
Sunlight plays perfect petals in symmetry array*

*Color and life bringing a bee to me
Pollen, my children availed to thee*

*Remember me and our summer shine
And I'll keep you close in this heart of mine*

Winter's Bite

Morning cold, windy bite
Needles and pins to skin so tight

Old Man Winter on a blow
Feels too cold for even snow

Bundle up with sweaters and hats
We all are looking like fat furry cats

Well though we complain of winter blast
In Florida we know this cold won't last

Tomorrow's high is seventy-nine!
Shorts and tee shirts and sandals time

Smile and remember winter's visit
But truth be told in Florida we don't miss it

El Niño Florida

*Morning sky is yellow the pool is green
Sure to be reminded it should really be clean*

*It's fall here, air and water should be cool and clear
As we lounge nearby with our cigars and beer*

*Working hard sweat rolls down my nose
Attacking mold with bleach and water hose*

*Green, black oh so stubborn clinging mold
Clean deck, clean pool, will it ever release its hold*

*Best times of the year are near: fall, winter, spring
If only El Niño would give up her stubborn cling*

*Oh well … maybe forget all this and go golfing instead
Out there I don't mind green nor sweat rolling off my head!*

Writer's Block

Poetry is elusive today for some reason
Maybe it's lazy, hazy summer season

Maybe all the connections aren't firing
Maybe it's my mind that is old and tiring

Well I don't know what to write about
Nothing in my mind that needs to come out

From my musing I'll give you a brief respite
Until I have something of interest to write

Our Friend the Moon

Our friend the moon will always be there
Even when you cannot see him shining there
Always and forever on our side he'll be there

Through clouds and shutters and shades he's there
Though ten thousand miles away shining he's there
Even if the jealous sun is shining brighter he's there

He was once one with Mother Earth
So he must always be there!

Alone Connecting with Me

*It's me alone in the mornings
I wonder of comings and goings*

*I listen to the air and enjoy artificial breeze
I read a little, clear my mind with a sneeze*

*I see and think of things as they really be
No interference or conversions made of me*

*I know what I like and who comes of mind
No strings or commitments yet to bind*

*Rising sun shines on gentle water shimmer
Hope for an ever better day just a glimmer*

*Horizon views and future dreams
A state of conscious wishes streams*

*With those dreams and thoughts alone
I feel connected to finally me alone*

Restlessness is a normal and yet sometimes an overcoming emotion. I've searched at times for inspiration. I've searched for meaning that I could write about, and at times, I realized the inspiration was to write about the despair of restlessness.

Restlessness

Restlessness prevails as time slows
Fear of life and living passing woes

Energy and thought direction fails
Activity without accomplishment sails

Where is my soul and muse today
Inspiration and direction in wild array

Like the boat tossed about in stormy sea
Maybe this writing really isn't my cup of tea

Ideas and passions surpass my norm
Thoughts and directions refuse to form

Do something, anything to make right
Maybe sunrise will end this dreadful night

Age and time are prevailing enemies now
Daring the waves I'm standing on the bow

No compass, direction, no port to find
Overcome time, ride the waves of my mind

Sunrise brings end to dreary night
Maybe soon I'll find port with aid of light

Spring is in the Air

Birds are chirping and playing
Trees and flowers blossom arraying

Soft breeze caresses flowers I see
Butterflies flutter oblivious of me

Clouds thin and so very light
Dance and change in sky alright

Bees are dancing all in a buzz
Pollen floats on breeze like fuzz

Here, there, everywhere is green
Including deck, patio, car I've seen

Here, there, everywhere a wheeze
Another, enjoying spring with a sneeze

A Summer's Day

Unexpectedly sky is so blue
Grass fresh and sweetly cut
In a tumble me and you

Sun always in shine
It's always down hill
For us there is no time

Fast we run and play
Ever young and free
On endless summer's day

Wind whistling a joyous tune
Sending dandelion fairies flying
This beautiful summer day in June

Tag you're it, now catch me
For I'll be back around again
For play and fun if you please

Adventures Sail

*Waves beat relentless upon the shore
Like a soft knock on adventure's door*

*Beckoning us to set sail out to sea
To places unknown for you and me*

*Leave the hustle of world behind
Look to the sea to really unwind*

*The wind, the waves, the salt air
Challenge the weather bad or fair*

*The wind and wire and sail singing
The feel of the tiller shudder and ringing*

*The tilt, the spray, the waves bounce
Going nowhere, and everywhere all at once*

*Controlling chaos, the wind obeys my will
Onward to adventure, until I get my fill*

*Then the alarm wakes me and I know
Just a dream I see, and back to work I go*

Sailing Along With Me

The wind and waves have a rhyme all their own
Angry, calm, always changing as present to me
My mind sails along adjusting always as one

I see and view and sing with all of thee
While second mind is working tiller and lines
Enchanted and mesmerized by the sea

Scooting along the water with haste
Nowhere to go, nowhere to be
Just we and the wind enjoying our race

Thank you for being along with me
Our souls wandering with the wind
This is how tranquility and peace should be

Riding High

Chancing extraordinary
Such fine and fickle winds
Suffering first occasioned loss

Lifted spirit flying
Rounding once again
Tenuous the line and hold

A slight movement
Exaggerated response
Down is up, up is down

Yet higher and beyond
Hearts do sing
With lines release

Seeking stability
Pulled even higher
Chasing extraordinary

Dreams

Ageless again I'll be
As time stands still
Night in my forest, it's me

Angels, demons and sages
A tug of war they play
In scenes of life's many pages

Joy, fears, inspirations they use
To win by making me believe
In this forested game of no rules

I hope the angels or sages win
Joy or inspiration in this timeless game
And not the demons from within

Dream in my forest where forever young is me
Dream in my forest where time knows no bounds
Dream in my forest and let's see who I'll be

Mother Earth

Mother Earth dancing into the night
Blue diamond shining beautiful and bright

Spinning graceful across the room
Watching in loving awe is Mr. Moon

Chasing the sun, leaning in and leaning out
Bringing seasons of life without a thought

Moon influences her emotions
Tides moving upon her oceans

Precious this diamond we call Mother
We who watch, draw loving life from her

She is strong no need to hold her hand
But be close to enjoy and protect her land

Her body of waters, so beautiful the sea
Keep her waters clear for you and me

She dances on, a graceful timeless soul
So fortunate for us as we must know

Another Night on the Road

Good night sleep 100 feet above the ground
7th floor for another night on road I'm found

Morning sun peeks in windows not shaded I see
I'm liking the gentle way the light wakes me

I hear the highway with thousands of chariots
... carrying working warriors to the fight
I hear the din of nearby rail yard and workers
....working trains that passed by screaming in the night

I think of my day and so many like this before
I think of the next and next and so much more

Join the rush just get out of bed
Shower and coffee will clear my head

Dropping in on Morning Rush Hour

Like a bird of prey we descend careful and slow
Sun high above, clouds here and down below

Lights barely seen through the haze
Houses and cars in suburban maze

Lights with halo mix with wet reflection
Our arrival causing no notice, no reaction

Flying into their world of morning hustle and run
Descending quietly, leaving the forgotten sun

Into the hazy, rainy, busy bustling day
Let me stay peaceful, above this fray

Football at Midnight

Stayed up way too late
Just to root for State

Network schedule bull
More games, all times full

Exciting back-n-forth game
Up, yes! Then if down it's a shame

Then with last score to win
Now just hold, don't let them in

No OT, its past my bedtime
No reviews and zebra dead time

Can barely, hang on and stay awake
Our team must win, so much at stake

At last however the other guys win
A home field loss it's a terrible sin

Good game, now finally off to bed
Tired, but now lie awake instead!

Scotch and Me

Heavens above blessed rain
Cool and clear refreshes the grain

By the river cool, clean and clear
Harvest my barley or rye my dear

Heat and time and I am one
Evaporate, filter, refine me home

Resting and thinking in barrels of oak
Soul maturing, complex I soak

Color of amber, made nice in a sherry cask
A little sweetness is not too much to ask

Complex and smooth I'll be just right
Enjoy me neat with a drop of rain tonight

A Little More

Taste is so enticing
A little more of course
With extra chocolate icing

A great feeling a great time
A little more of course
It makes for a fun rhyme

Beautiful music, terrific score
A little more of course
Please come back for that encore

Your thoughts, ideas so neat
A little more of course
Share your mind without repeat

A hug from you so sweet
A little more of course
It makes me feel complete

Shhh!

A day sunny and bright
Or rainy and dark like night

So much to do or maybe not
It might be cold or maybe hot

A weekend's quiet afternoon
Or workday getting away soon

Any way you look at it by me
A glorious afternoon it can be

With just a little nap time
That can be all mine o'mine

Symmetry in Five-Word Lines

See harmony, beauty in words
Symmetry of balance this affords

Left side, right side balance
Keep us centered without dissidence

Justice is symmetry of fair
Good, bad in the air

Hear the music beautiful sound
Build up then swing down

See harmony in the dance
Mirrored movement in a trance

Lovely symmetry in her eyes
Heart soars into the skies

Find symmetry in your world
Beauty is sure to unfurl

If I Could Dream on Cue

If I could only dream on cue
I think I'd dream of me and you

Would you like what I dream
Or be confused by my subconscious stream

On a ship at sunset sail
Or on a morning's nature trail

Would you come along with me
I'll tell you stories of land and sea

I'll tell you inner thoughts and battles won
As we roll in grass of summer's midday sun

Would you like what you'd hear
And care to know dreams so clear

Maybe you'd rather have dreams alone
Dreams of your thoughts featured and shone

If I could only dream on cue
Or rather join a dream with you

Water and You

Dew adorned grass, wet feet
Tickle our toes, as we meet

Rain, thunder and lightning
Light and dark so enlightening

Leaves, flowers and so many trees
Storing water and spring beauty please

Waves spray sweet cool, until
Goosebumps showing our chill

Refreshing, floating so lazy
Inspiring thoughts go hazy

Bubbles, jets at a hundred and four
Warming hearts and inspiring more

For making fine whiskey and wine
Cheering your health as well as mine

For life is better with you
And life-giving water too!

A Field of Black and White

Enthroned on a field of black and white
To do strategic battle for what is right

For the moment queen is close at my side
Evaluating all the risks arrayed on the other side

Bounding and maneuvering knights
Travel forward looking for fights

Pawns inch forward and sacrifice
Too easily their least-valued lives

Bishops dressed in religious garbs
Cast sideways glances with sharp barbs

Rooks late to battle, and castle protect
Reserves for later power project

The queen flits easily forward and back
She manages intrigue and leads the attack

A game of thrones with a hobbled king
Moving nearly like a pawn, with little sting

Two dimensions and so many options
Think ahead many thoughtful notions

View the field from on high
As a bird would float and fly

Lure your adversary into a trap today
Or surprise with a brilliant unexpected play

A game of war, of strategy and of might
Played on a field of black and white

There's always tomorrow....

Maybe Tomorrow I will

Seize the day or carpe diem
Live with vitality and purpose
Put regrets and worries on the shelf
Think of blessings and joys
Find that energy and drive
Oh my … maybe tomorrow I will!

Christmas Throughout the Year

*I know a happy soul that always whistles a Christmas tune
He whistles just as happily regardless if it's December or June*

*For him Christmas joy is not for a certain time of year
Rather it is an everyday spirit through his whistle we hear*

*If only Christmas was all the time
Then love and peace would forever shine*

*It's not the decorations, the presents under the tree
But our time with friends and family we love to see*

*If only Christmas was all throughout the year
Then children would never know a single tear*

*It's not the stores, the elves and Santa we need
We need the joy and spirit of God's grace indeed*

*If only Christmas' perfect meaning was clear
In our hearts, it must live throughout the year*

*And if you get a chance, especially in June
I hope you'll whistle your own joyous Christmas tune!*

I've traveled a lot on business, and every once in awhile it's unavoidable. It's cold season and you've got to get back home, and the only way is to tough it out on a flight. You know that everyone hates you and can't stand to be near you, but there you are. Sometimes you are just that dude in 9C.

I'm the Dude in 9C

You know they are looking at me
I feel their thoughts, I hope he's not near me
There's a seat open, and it's 9C
I plop my bags, and manage the overhead
The sideways glances the lean away is evident
I've planned ahead, as much as I could do
I look ahead, no eye contact is part of the plan
I've got medications to help
I've got napkins, they hold up better than tissue
I've got four hours of closeness with
9B and 9D and rows 8 and 10
Fruitlessly I suppress cough, it just makes it worse
You know it has to come out–I might just explode
It sounds worse than it is, but who's going to want to hear that
I know what they are thinking anyway, my next week is ruined
I hope not, but I couldn't drive home, so there's no choice
Sometimes it's a bit of life's lottery, sorry you were near 9C
Finally, arrival, and for a first, no one crowds me as I leave
They never stopped looking at me

Feet up at the End of the Day

When you've fought the battle well
When it's of success you wish to tell
And pride causes your chest to swell

Celebrate accomplishment with a happy smile
Put your feet up at the end of the mile
Let your toes flag fly for a little while

What is That Dollar Worth?

If you see a dollar lying on the ground
Would you be happy about what you found

Would you set that dollar once again free
On something shiny and new that you see

Is it worth less than the one you've earned
And if so what have you really learned

The dollar knows no difference from its brother
It's you that have assigned character to the other

One dollar that is found is fun and furious
The dollar earned and saved seems so serious

What is that dollar worth to you
And do you like its brother equally too?

It Must be Here

It must be here, somewhere
I just cannot see it, I swear

Open my mind, it must be here
Close now, search, it is near

More effort, more thought
The desire, driven, sought

Remember like in a dream
Toss and turn in sub-conscience stream

Cannot feel calm nor rested
Cannot quit, cannot be bested

There a glimpse, just beyond
Encouraging, urging me on

It's there in all its perfection
Then turn and lost connection

The glimpse, the taste, entice
Maze-like the world to the mice

It must be somewhere, someday
And I'll be there somehow, someway

My Friend the Trees

Hello trees big and tall
Hello trees leaves and all

I know what you would like
To take a walk, to make a hike

But I ask you here to stay
On this bright and sunny day

I love to nap in shade of trees
If you'll just stay here pretty please

I will happily build a pen
Just to keep my trees in

Then I know I'll see all of them
My friends the trees, when I awaken

Dance and shake with wind
Just don't wander away again

Thank you trees!

Just a Boat Tied by the Sea

*Where the sea caresses the sand
Held from wander tied to this land
Bounce and wave testing bounds
The birds, the breeze and calling sounds
Left to neglect of wind and time
Tiring, failing losing shine
Green and decaying energy gone
Strands in the wind sing a sad song
Eventually ties no longer hold
But there's nothing left and nowhere to go*

Fall's Coming!

Summer is tired and worn
Hot and humidity forlorn

Boring, little relief, rerun groans
Thankful for summer Game of Thrones

Our team's boringly out of the race
Since All-star game, they've been off the pace

Football excitement coming soon
Weekends busy all thru an afternoon

Tired of wet and summer's evergreen
Color our fall memories we have seen

Coolness and hopeful dry
With beautiful and clear sky

Come-on fall, drive away summer's swoon
I'm sure we'll call on spring sometime soon!

Musician's Passion

One evening during dinner and drinks, I watched, impressed by great and beautiful music being delivered to a room that barely paid attention. Certainly as background it stirs hearts and minds as music must do, but the passion to drive it forward in spite of remarkable distraction was amazing, and I saw it as an interesting metaphor for persistence and passion in life....

Musician's Passion

A hundred eat, drink as they mingle
Music floats gently above them all
Stirring hearts and minds just a single

People lost to points they must make
Servers ply their food and drink for tips
Passion drives him forward for music sake

Surely he notices but never seems to care
Dishes, glasses, silver ringing odd notes
Purity, clarity of music emotion he tries to share

Nourished by infrequent applause scattered
He drives the music with passion and talent
Happy he plays, their attention never mattered

Witness this beautiful metaphor for life
He persists as he must, nourished by few
His passion for music overcoming all strife
He smiles ... and so do we who know life is good!

Karaoke

I sit and nurse a drink and watch with amusement
I think that human history is resplendent with refinement in fermentation
Drink forever a magnificent fuel for social engagement
Surely the history of and primal need for song must parallel that of drink
But what damage could you do around the campfire, or hearth I wonder
While I listen to friends in low places, where whiskey drowns, and beer chases, I ponder
That a century ago, Edison brings us the microphone along with lights
And the Japanese, naturally industrialize it all
I can only hope everyone here has had enough to drink
And that Jimmy Buffett forgives me when I lay waste to Margaritaville
It has come to my turn at the karaoke mike…
I blew out my flip flop, stepped on a pop top
Cut my heel, had to cruise on back home
But there's booze in the blender…

Part 2:
The World as I See It

I believe that poetry is an interesting and historically significant means to express our world and realities, the beautiful and wonderful as well as the ugly and sorrowful. As an observer of world and country and civilization, many emotions, thoughts and insights come to mind and are brought forward here. Yes, some of this may be viewed as political because it is often about people and the influence of people, which is the general intent of poetry. I expect that in many cases the reader may have views that differ from mine. I expect that many will not agree with my messages, and I respect that. However, I'm not going to argue nor explain, just present the world as I see it and hope that it broadens horizons of thought.

Migration

More people are migrating and are refugees of war or corruption or gang violence and conflict at this time than any time since World War II. In the US, about 46M people are immigrants (they were born in a different country), some estimated 11M are illegally here. Europe continues to see an influx of millions of refugees, and immigration is a dominant issue. Worldwide, the estimate of immigrant population is 255M. Consider that too many are moving not for advancement and careers but rather to escape corruption, violence and conflict.

I shudder to think of the implications if too many millions lose hope....

When Night Becomes Most Dark

Escaping nightmare or chasing a dream
Into a desert or fording a stream

Tears and perils and threats
From anxiety, strife and regrets

No option, no option, move on
Stay and die or live on the run

Footprints of thousands before
Bloodied knuckles on the door

No attorney, no help, no money
Just move on, hoping for land of milk and honey

Returned and we'll try again
There's nowhere else to land

Millennia of refugees, moving on rumor
No love, no life, no soul, no humor

Where to run if left without hope
Turn to find society's slippery slope

Where is revolution's kindling and spark
Where the night becomes most dark

Life's Lottery

Families caught in crossfire of war
Walking beyond endurance to find some semblance of safety
Tragically short of food, medicine and water
Through checkpoints of soldiers unknown
Language differences, tribal boundaries
Constant fear, constant stress
For soldiers too, weary, no clarity
Children are bombers, and enemies are indistinct from victims
Life's lottery brings some pain and suffering and stress
Bring to others safety, opportunity, liberty and happiness
We who won this lottery should be forever grateful

Inspired by the Grapes of Wrath...

They Seeded our Future

Then the rains blew through but not for us
The earth cracked and paled and loosened
We waited, watched and figured unjust

The winds came and lifted the dirt
The sky was dark the sun didn't show
The air was thick and stinging it hurt

The tenuous hold of prosperity our land
Banks know but not care of soil no longer
Time to leave and escape this desert sand

In bucking junk of a truck, lucky ones leave
Others walk or hitch or rail must ride
To a paradise, a promised land of lush and leaf

The road is hard, some will fail, others die
There is no certainty only hope to drive us on
No one looks back just move, shrug and sigh

Millions of others too demand a chance
Just like we, need a place to work and earn
A place to teach, learn and even to dance

But sorrow and difficulty like never before
The fields are controlled and pay is meager
We buy what we can from company store

Hunger is every day, this migrant life of hell
Organize for safety and wages if you can
Survive beatings, floods and keep children well

We are needed soon, a call to action bell doth toll
We will rise up above for a world's higher cause
We will feed each other, give sustenance to the soul

We are a precursor to a fairer world, a better life
One which we and our children must earn
With blood, sweat, incredible toil and strife

Some days are not so good....

Migraine

Image perfect and clear
Now splintered, or wet
Jagged confused, pain too near

Mad at disrupt of day
Of mind's perfect betrayal
Forcing an all stop and stay

Find quiet, find dark
See mind electric
Seek calm, control spark

Simple mind matters
Failure is great pain
Loss leaves me in tatters

Knife shatters all peace
Stomach erupts
Breathe, hope it will ease

Vision back, but I don't want to see
Stay in dark, quiet
Manage pain and just try to breathe

Always hours, maybe five
Hang on and live
Get there, just survive

Brutal, life stress affects
Try to control, or accept
It's just one of many defects

Fever's Hold on Me

*Shiver, shake, sweat clothes, bedding bundle
Back and forth tossing, turning and tumble*

*Every muscle, even bones seem to ache
Sweat, shiver, how many hours will this take*

*Mind race, to and from decisions made
Back again, no order so decisions unmade*

*Think of everyone and no-one I know
Think of everything to do, when and how*

*Turn and toss sweat and ache even more
Moments lucid, then lost behind fever's door*

*Round and round a wrap of clothes bind
Round and round a wrap of confused mind*

*Hours of torture over, body finally tamed
Oh this cold this fever finally named*

*Coming back down to earth in this puddle
But my mind no longer lost and befuddle*

*Feverish night is like insanity in view
I hope it is a long time before another flu*

So, You Want my Vote

I'm a citizen, tell me something of note
If you have the gall to ask for my vote

Don't tell me the others are not safe
Don't tell me of news that's really fake

Let's hear the vision you have for us
Or don't bother to lecture us

We are not fools that believe just anything
We are life busy, so be clear and say something

Why can't there be a true debate
Instead of all this yelling and hate?

Why don't we respect each other
And not hide truth from one-another?

And when you get there to fulfill your oath
Why would you pound your chest and boast?

The reason you're there is to serve
Not to gloat about something you don't deserve

Work with each other, make a future of note
Don't just battle and position for my next vote!

Mountain Reckoning

The mountain draws us ever close
Majestically demanding its own prose

Dramatically urging an attempting
Come, get higher, summit tempting

Always there with perspective sight
Grand vista's reward the brave, the right

Ah, but that climb is oh so steep
The strength needed ever deep

Paths often so unclear
The top vanishingly near

Mankind, tribes, nations climb
A must to find a better place in time

Born in a valley we are drawn to heights
Struggles, growth, learning and fights

It is a life of strain, of stress of battle scars
Yet our souls seek this path to the stars

The mountain is always there beckoning
Our drive and character it's always reckoning

Incredible that children would be attacked with chemical weapons, that families are driven from their homes and are bombed unmercifully. I cried when I wrote this….

Tears for Aleppo

War is a shame
We so easily claim

But it is our shame that we must own
Is our human-less soul hard as stone?

We watch a disaster unfold from afar
Following our knowing, self-righteous shining star

We complain of crimes, of sins unimagined
But we knew, empty threats, empty promises damage

Abandoned our brothers, sisters, children too
To another monster of power in the East, and you know who

We claim to be weary, even claim to have won
We saved ourselves, and precious red-lined drawn

But now what of the millions on the road?
What of horrors that are still to be told?

What of the children that cry though the night?
What would our shame and tears make right?

Can we look away, distracted by our stars?
Can we enjoy our world and ignore the scars?

Look straight at the world as it really is
Look at the children as they die for soul-less ideals

And if you can easily claim
War is just an ugly shame?

Then too find a moment to shed a tear
For all those still living in absolute fear!

At the time of the Parkland Florida High School Shooting, it occurred to me that possibly gun control is as much a matter of attention span as it is about the will we have to make changes.

What a Waste

Beautiful, young, future's many and strong
Possible artists, doctors, inventors, and heroes
We'll never know what they may have accomplished
We'll never know the good they may have done
If they'd succeed in life, even if they'd make our lives different
All because they died going to the movies,
going to church, to a concert
And maybe worst of all because they were
bettering themselves in school
We light candles, and pray, and say what a shame it is
We hear of heroes that shield others through tears of pain
Then we go on with our day
What can we do, what can we say?
Memorials and flowers and teddy bears,
remembrances, until it rains
And in November we'll vote again
without remembering their names

An Accident at Rush Hour

An accident at rush hour, 7 cars
Inconvenient for many, tragic for some
Our baby in the middle, but she's able to call
She's injured in the ambulance, fear as we arrive
She's bruised and cut and as we extract her and
    go to the hospital
Others are being lifted into ambulances and glass
    is being swept
The cause was a woman, drunk, distracted, a storm of
    uncertainty
She's at the hospital as we wait, along with her man, trying
    to explain
No point in listening, no need to respond, a reckless storm
    knows no guilt
Lives disrupted, maybe permanent, maybe tragically, but
    the storm won't remember
It's just an accident at rush hour, something to find
    your way around
Unless it's you, your loved ones, that are trying to
    weather the storm
The storm will blow through and tragically do it again
No responsibility, there's insurance for that
Haul the cars away, clean the mess
Pray the victims will rebuild from this storm!

Pick-up Baseball

Just a lad of about five or six, mom said enough, now go play
I knew of a park just two blocks away
I rode my bike, dad had just taught me how to ride without training wheels
Not really a park, it was land carved out under the power lines
Early summer, and there are kids gathering around a makeshift field
Rocky base path worn in the grass, nothing more
A fence that defines the edge of the so-called park
Some swings and a monkey bar in the corner that no one paid attention to
A cylinder or two of huge concrete pipes, that judging by graffiti someone cared about
Hey kid, do you want to play baseball?
Sure….
Are you left or right handed?
I don't know?
They toss me a ball I try to catch with my left, drop it and throw it back
They said I was right handed, and gave me a glove for my left-hand, which confused me
A bat was tossed, and an older boy and older girl picked up sides
Nervous I waited and was finally picked last and sent to right field
But that didn't make sense either I was on the left side of the field where they told me to stand

I loved playing, I loved that they figured out how to make up teams, and everyone was welcome, this game of baseball was incredible.
We played there for a few years, as I got older, I eventually was picking teams
I was telling a new kid where to stand in right field
No-one really cared who won, only that we had the joy of playing for hours
I played until I hit a homerun over the fence and clobbered a car one day
It was time to move to a bigger field, wear uniforms and play

Beneath a Scarlet Sky… is an incredible story of a hero and tragic love loss

The following poem is inspired by a book of the same name, written by Mark T. Sullivan, who tells the incredible but true story of an Italian boy Pino Lella, who grows up during World War II to become a hero many times over but in the process tragically loses his true love.

Beneath a Scarlet Sky

Adventure and life oblivion of youthful insight
Interrupting us on this unforeseeably violent night

That sky with lights, with burning fires
Scarlet, tortured, indecent death pyres

Escape, survive, action for the fleeing loving others
Learn, strengthen, flying with our roman brothers

Bravely in love, bravely in service of right
Fragility of life exposed, of wit, of action into the night

Of secrets, of hidden lives, of scarlet skies
Careful, learn again, keep the secret with vital lies

Of love of culture, country, of love of life of each other
Where can we be, what can we do, dear brother

Death always at the door, life and love short
Nowhere to run, never to find a safe port

Fight with cunning and information and wile
Living in the moment, seeing all, biting back the bile

The evil and the weak die without honor or shame
And still the brave and innocent die ugly all the same

Guilt of survival, heartbreak driven revenge
Keep it together, cannot allow this mind to unhinge

More in a few years than anyone should see
So much more life to live so much more to be

But how to go beyond, how to find your heart
How to forever live for what has fallen apart

In Honor of Miosotis Familia...

Miosotis Familia was a 48-year-old mother of 3, and herself the youngest of 10 children from a Dominican Republic family that immigrated to New York. She was tragically killed, assassinated, because she was a police officer working in the Bronx. There is significant danger for those who choose an occupation with the intent to protect us, the public, and to ensure our nation is a nation of laws and civility. We should be forever grateful to all those who risk their lives to protect us.

In Honor of Miosotis Familia

Love, laughter, a family, a future
She dreamt and worked to ensure

And to a higher commitment of a civil cause
Never expecting glory, recognition or applause

A commitment to another family of blue
With oath of service, keeping the peace for me and you

Knowing danger, knowing pain
Out there, in snow, heat or rain

Risking daily for our safety and peace
Fear, tension that can never cease

You who's made the ultimate sacrifice
Who's given more than anyone could ask

For you and your family we do pray
As well your family of blue still in danger every day!

Patriot's Ideals

Ideals defined by thought and design
Those words become one with us
Forever fair and free in heart and mind

Committed complete and with resolve
To share, care, protect and nurture
Never weak or slow to problem-solve

With higher purpose and with pride
Protecting our freedoms, doing what's right
Onto the challenge, into the fire we do ride

Whenever wherever those colors do fly
There too are the thoughts and words
Meaning and purpose no one can deny

Through this creation of freedom air
Our patriot's words and deeds ensure
A nation, a people beyond compare

Our united ideals were always right
Learning, welcoming, understanding
America's past, present and future's bright

I was thinking about the ones who are not given a chance, of the ones who find themselves cut-off prior to their shot at life, a sadness that is beyond compare and yet too unfair to those who live with the implication of no choice, no chance.

No Chance

It's quiet I've just heard
It's a vision I never saw
Of a future that will never occur

I know a past that has not arisen
And its life that'll never be lived
A perfect soul totally misgiven

My chance, my shot not taken
Lived life without a breath
All because I was mistaken

Workers' Struggle

Our country discusses immigration in terms of security and numbers, and yet what is it for those who are poor, who live to work because they must? I, fortunate of education and opportunity, enjoy the time of leisure, time of contemplation. Even when I struggled to find success, there was always time for being one with myself. Can I imagine the honor, the duty to family, to a life as an immigrant itinerant worker, and yet how as intelligent soulful beings they must struggle with "today's" existence and defer those thoughts of being one in body, mind and soul?

Body, Mind and Soul

My body and mind are thrown into this toil
Tied by duty, honor and life to this soil

I've been here before a thousand times
My body works to a certain rhythm and rhyme

I know the field, I know the tools, and soil so well
My hands, my head are one at work with no tell

It bends, it aches, life poured into today's existence
Yet the soul and heart knows life at a distance

Let my mind, my heart, my soul drift free
Let them not interfere with what I must do and be

Hold on through this day, hold on to all small victories won
Hold on for the time when heart, mind and soul are one

Feel the rain, hear the thunder, it's part of a plan
Fight on, toil on, this is a must, because we can

Heart and soul are where they must be
Because these things are born to be free

Hold on to me, Lord, hold on till kingdom come
Where once again heart, mind, body and soul are one

I Had a Friend

I had a friend, lively, smart, quick with a smile
But he could be distant, gone at times for awhile

He was brilliant as any I knew when he tried
But his mother worried, and sometimes cried

Was he quiet, pensive or just tired today
Was he joyous, active and funny the other day

Go get him up, help him, get him going please
With prodding with challenge, and game's tease

Then we are grown, and worlds apart, all new
Education, families, careers, calls become few

But who will fix him when in depths broken
Friends, family or others, with words spoken

Then a child battles sickness for years
In the fight, everything in, including tears

Death catches and brings tragedy unimaginable
How can any mortal overcome, inconsolable

I want to help to get him up and going again
But he is broken and unable to let go of pain

His world collapses into a smaller space
Unavailable always, friends cannot make a case

A rising star passes, and father's smile doth end
I share the pain and sadly also lost a friend

Part 3:
Philosophy and Me

A long time ago, high school to be precise, I started to think about the world, possibly like all teenagers, or maybe a little different than others, I cannot know. I started to question traditions, religion, and what I had been told. I felt like there was some truth in all that I saw in religion, in traditions and in the wisdom of authors I found interesting. But all that I was reading and all that I observed couldn't be true. There were contradictions. Some were called mysteries and matters of faith. I decided that reasoning mattered. I read the bible and found that it made no sense to me unless I read deeper and tried to understand the message behind the stories, as if it was poetry with layers of meaning. I felt that it should be right to question and discuss and consider deeper truths.

I was surprised when a teacher in high school turned to me one day in class, and said, "Let's hear what Socrates has to say." It was embarrassing at the time, as I knew this would be a nickname that would stick.

Many years later, I found a used book in a basket of books for sale and bought Plato's *The Last Days of Socrates*. I learned about the Socratic Method, which involves creating a theory and then questioning it until contradictions are uncovered—a way of thinking and reasoning that makes great sense.

Socrates also was a contributor to the Stoic Philosophy, which I've also read about, including Marcus Aurelius' book *Meditations* (yes, the Roman Emperor). He was remarkable in his embrace of Christian-like principles while simultaneously persecuting Christians.

Sincerely

Mysterious at first as I try
To reach across and ask
Frighten then calm I realize

Move seamlessly among them all
Listen carelessly, but searching
Then onward beyond the wall

Searching as Diogenes did
For something, someone sincere
Where true intentions never hid

When I find a virtuous track
I listen to see if its circumstance or time
Causes of one or many topple the stack

I give a nudge, carefully if I might
Encouraging the sincerest road
I know they feel if only slight

I listen and get the occasioned lie
For if it helps others, of course
If sincerity in such intent does not die

What matters it really seems
Is sincerely to know one's self
Not believing those fanciful dreams

Finding purpose in life in-between
Pushing toward small victorious joy
Sincerity intent often going unseen

Wisdom

Wisdom whispers to us
Why's it so hard to hear her?
My world is so noisy
Yet I know she is there
She is breathtaking panoramic, and
I'm looking at the smallest details
She is intricate in her fine work
I can't see the message in the picture

She speaks through the meek
I listen to the proud
The wise add ideas, but
Are drowned by the chant of many

She stands at my bed in the mid of the night
I'm too tired to capture the thoughts
Please speak to me through my day
I promise I'll listen in my own way

What do you Believe?

Do you believe in what you see
Then does magic and sleight of hand deceive
Do you believe the stories you've been told
Does it matter if it's Hollywood or sacred books of old
Do you think of thoughts deep
Or just dream when you sleep
Can you feel something you cannot see
Do you understand what you barely perceive
What of that whisper in the wind
Do you hear that message sent
Is there more to us than this
What if belief is what we miss
What if beyond is not there
Does it matter should we care
If love and thought be our legacy
Will it be etched on our effigy
What now do you believe
Hopefully much more than you see

Both of Me

Defined this one by what I do
But what does it mean to you

Is it accomplishment you see
Or the other person I've come to be

Two minds working side by side
Trying to balance life's bumpy ride

Is relevance now in the past
Will accomplishments really last

Understand this from where you are
The only way to see is from afar

Too close you find us two
Easy to confound and confuse

Conflict unbalanced by change
Priorities, thoughts rearrange

Energetic me is forever younger
The other me somewhat stronger

Yin and yang of who we are
Bringing peace and sometimes war

Building of Logic

So clear the words but not the thought
Clear the emotion unexpected nor sought

Feeling, tasting, the scent of logic sweet
In minds and words, we may then meet

Challenge truths without selfish emotion
No salve, no need for soothing lotion

Question the stairs, the rooms, the doors
Building of logic, hidden truth in stores

But at times others cannot follow
Proceeding without, I did when I was callow

Now it seems those truths hidden deep
Are fine and fair to know, but not keep

They remain as they are
To me close and never far

But for those truths hard to take
We play with words for illusion's sake

Rounded

Remember bubbles wonderful and round
Strength and beauty in round to be found

Arch supports builder's dream
Rounded by pi and so very clean

Orbits of gravity efficiency
Life modesty and sufficiency

Heavenly bodies in perfect sphere
Be in the moment, be right here

Hands mark time in a circle face
Everything is right in time and place

A well-rounded life is sure to be
The best of life for you, you'll see

This Poem Writes Itself

*Shuttered and rest easy
No light, no dark, no thought
Feel the light and hear breezy*

*Where are we on this morn
Nowhere, not here nor there
Hear a fair and waking horn*

*In my subconscious streams
In my mindless thoughts
Chasing clouds and dreams*

*In distant words and pages
Stories, poems and books
Literary ideas from the ages*

*Birthing ideas slow and unsure
Toddler learning to walk
No ideas yet fully mature*

*Philosophy and theology
Twisted vines of same genius
Limited by this poor biology*

*A poor poet brings nothing home
The work writes itself
If it is to be alive and be a poem*

*A service of love in time
To let the words out on page, and
Bring it together in fortunate rhyme*

Changes

*At times head and heart
Can be very far apart*

*Life changes are not alone
Others affected or seeds sown*

*Change is a measure of life
And yet can cut like a knife*

*Know thyself, thyself be true
Others in change are not you*

*Memories are of the past
Good and bad they will last*

*Remember the best of them
Giving up on least of them*

*Embrace the future change brings
Bring with the best of past things*

Of Love, Wisdom and Truth

Born to this world with all hope and possibility
Nurtured and developed with love of family
Dependent on all and yet we grow in passion

Passion for all we need and want and smiles shared
Giving way in time to hope and desire of what's to be
We determine our way, our path in life and love

Or rather is our path set before us with options here and there
Are the directions and decisions determined by our wisdom
Or are they choices driven by a collective wisdom of society

Does humanity develop a collective wisdom aged and advanced generationally
What be that social fabric that conveys that wisdom— religion, science, art, literature
That fabric wears and tears and requires repair and renewal in time

We connect our inner being and soul to this fabric, this wisdom
It's easier to find comfort in this all-knowing wisdom without reason
When we wander through and test the fabric do we advance or damage

Wonderment and open hearts make for wise souls
Worn and torn fabric is obligated our attention and repair
But it is easy to be content with histrionic protections of failed fabric

Learning is a wonderful way to pursue the corners of wisdom for value
Yet to learn along the paths set before us throughout the fabric of humanity
Or better yet to advance learning beyond the fabric and into creation

Our children, our future generations will be opened to a greater wisdom
Our understanding of social fabrics that carry ideas, thoughts and passion
We play a role that is beyond our horizon of sight, beyond our life and love

Our logic and reasons cannot reconcile with the areas of the social fabric at times
Thus pushing us as far as hate of such dullards of humanity that embrace this fabric
We forget that this same fabric is part of our weave too and for many their only comfort

In our mind, logic screams this must change!
We desire to improve and repair as we can in our corner of mankind
Yet the others hold to that blanket with a maniacal unreasoned grip

The truths they hold in their unreasoned grip seem absolute to the believer
The investigator sees these truths to be relative to the perspective of observer

Seeking to uncover that core value and wisdom that drove need for absolutism

These truths then create a prison of absolutism that restricts freedom
Choking life, love and thought from adherents of mismanaged fabric
Yet giving false power and judgmental superiority to the advocators and enforcers

Shall we embrace these challenges to logic as they are encountered
Shall we tolerate what is comfort to others, allow to live and let live
Doesn't reason drive us to compassionate learning and tolerance of their comfort

We have a responsibility to learn, teach and nurture compassionately
To advance the fabric or to leave it unmolested requires application of wisdom
To act without thought and to base on prejudice is an act against wisdom and love

Freeing our minds and hearts allows passions of imagination beyond constraints
The social fabric of our reasoned soul cannot constrain our imagination
Love like a dove soars easily above the fabric of convention and tradition

As a dove released from the weighted constraints of local monochromatic fabric
We soar above the quilted plane and see the many colors and textures of life
This gift of living perspective allows us to grow in wisdom, love and truth

With wisdom we build a legacy of smiles by bringing new worlds to those we influence
We can expand thought and help each other see beauty with perspective
We can point out beauty, point to the moon and sunrise and say appreciate it my friend

There is little more beautiful than God's gift of this world we live on
Our star, our support system, and
Those that came before, building society, language, arts, science

We are entertained like no one before, we live like Gods
We have an obligation to contemplate and investigate our fabric and our legacy
How we share, how we love determines what "legacy" we leave this world

The Other Side

So, I find myself on the other side it seems
Couldn't imagine, never in my dreams

Never in the middle, never in between
Not here before, not sure what I mean

Flying into the endless sunset
Delaying that night comes yet

Thoughts wheel in the sky
Like starlings way on high

Escaping above, beyond is dying
Surely no more pain, no sighing

But there I find on the other side
Wisdom and beauty of this ride

Unlocking the Door

Thoughts and freedom under lock and key
Madness hides behind the door you see

Do these thoughts deserve the light of day
Is it safe, is it complex, dangerous to say

Is complexity or confusion of thought value given
Open this door to examine heart and soul's haven

Is it valued or worse yet, no one does care
These inner workings of a mind to share

Is it over-wrought value, loneliness or more
If you get this, do you expect there's more in store

Can I put this away and lock it up again
Incarcerate and avoid any chance of pain

Or shall I leave it open and toss the key
Finding vulnerable what's there of me

Whispers on the Wind

If your heart be open and your mind be free
Could you then understand someone like me

If I really listen careful to whisper on the wind
Would I know what is in your heart just then

Fear, joy, love and proud can they be understood today
Across the room or many miles with no discerned delay

If it is faith, or if it is intuition, is it perception, or simply love
Life's emotion lives barely perceived like rustle
from wings of a dove

Nature is resplendent with diversity, beauty and mystery
Be one with this nature and take in time, this point of history

For time is this point and future unknown,
and past sins please relieve
Be in the moment and know what we know
and allow our hearts to believe

We are connected by time, by nature and
by whispers on the wind
Believe and then you'll understand and
know the loving message I send

Keep Her Close

Quiet, thinking, in stillness I sat
Waiting for what, one could ask

For revelations, waiting for why
Impossible in youth I cannot deny

As if pondering life-long mysteries
And challenging Byzantine-like histories

Why we are who we are
How we came this far

Where we go from here
Is there nothing we should fear

Control and shaped a world to our liking
Conquered with the deftness of a Viking

Yet she too waits, planning her future wins
If we forget, go too far, commit too many sins

Keep thinking, there is harmony in sight
Secrets of life, joining with mother nature is right

Keep her close, respect her needs
Future ensured with carefully planted seeds

If a man does not master his circumstances, then he is bound to be mastered by them....

Dancing with Circumstance

*Our minds see us not as we are
But as we wish, and often from afar
So too, we view our circumstance
As if just a partner in delicate dance
But no partner to be controlled
She dances to music, unheard, untold
She occupies the spaces she desires
It is we who respond, as she inspires
We may want desperately to succeed
But rarely, so rarely she lets us lead
To music we find our way across floor
To see if and where we may find a door
But alas we are not going anywhere*

Listen and Learn

Words spoken for all to hear
Meaning to see it a little more clear

Listen with both your eyes and ears
See excite, love and even fears

Suspend beliefs, open closed minds
Amazing and amassing new finds

Sometimes wisdom in a whisper found
A world away but homeward bound

Not all you see is absolute and true
Don't believe all heard by others or you

Learning to listen, learning to discern
Wisdom from nonsense can be learned

Wisdom grows with mistakes and age
Turn and read on to the next page

But learning never is over or done
There's a higher place, another rung

Read and listen, learn and discuss
In your developing wisdom learn to trust

When You Were Eleven

Remember you as a child of eleven,
… needs and wants and desires
In the present and beyond into future fires

So much is a given, so much is form
What we do fits a pattern, a norm

You look beyond, go beyond current path
Ignoring reality's cruel math

Imagining, a future perfect now
It will be different someway somehow

But it is the journey, the effort the way
Giving you joy, if you accept it every day

There is always a future, always a desire
Always a path, a struggle, another fire

You may not see it complete or fair
But someday you know when you are there

As life brings you that little bit of heaven
Think how far you've come since you were just eleven

Elusiveness of Tranquility

Why is it difficult sometimes to find tranquility
Is it beyond our meager mental ability

We journey through our limited time
With useless worry of future on our mind

In the sometimes lonely, in mid of night
We feel futility of struggle and fight

We realize solemnity of existence
In the limits of time's distance

Some would pray for relief
To an unseen God, or mysterious belief

We seek kindred spirits to share
Our anxiety and honesty if we dare

Or we find comfort in a drink
So to sleep and not to think

Maybe tranquility and peace, we will reach
On some faraway shore and sandy beach

Or in our love's and heart's mind at night
We find our soul's truth and know it's right

My Forest

Woke early this morning wondering if I was still me
Would I know or would I care if myself I could not see

I tossed and turned with some worry and concern
For what reason today I could not discern

A hurricane of thoughts running through my mind
A worry I didn't do, didn't say enough for them to find

If I were lost, would you look in this forest behind every tree
Would you risk what you might find and what you might see

In the forest of thick and heavy wood
Be gentle with what you find if you should

I find that there is so much learning possible if we only embrace our natural curiosity. When we were children, we asked why and wondered about so much, and as we mature we sometimes allow that wonder to wander away from us. We learn what we must to become productive in this world. That is often a given for most who will be reading these pages. However, the world is much more interesting and there is much we can benefit in our lives, our careers and within ourselves if we just run with curiosity.

Loving Curiosity

Let her free, she will then be your friend
Curiosity will be with you until the end

She will guide you in lifelong learning
Love her if it's wisdom you're yearning

Forget salaciousness of celebrity and Hollywood stars
Forget triviality of rumored family and friend's scars

This world of nature, science, math and beautiful art
Of literature, history, and genius we must never part

There is so much to learn, and she can teach us
If we let her, and we listen to world wondrous

Thinking About It

Thinking is the feeling of a thought
The consideration of all sides
Saying it as simply as possible
Rare and improbable are unique thoughts
All thoughts are vulnerable if shared
But opened and shared thoughts are the most intimate of human actions
And thoughtlessness is the death of feeling and therefore inhumane
Keep thinking!

Keep it Simple … Some Thoughts….

It's complex to make things simple … corollary is, it's easy to make simple things complex
Occam's razor postulates that the theory with the fewest assumptions is most often the correct one
Poetry that people like the best is simple
I used to think that telling me that my poetry is deep was a compliment
Complexity can be your friend, but simple is better understood
I sleep easier with clarity and conviction of simple than I do with complex inventions
The essence of a simple problem seems to enjoy being wrapped in complexity

Simply said … have a great day!

Of Perspective and Shading

I read a great book about Leonardo da Vinci by Walter Isaacson that is quite interesting. Leonardo da Vinci was obsessed with and investigated the geometries of perspective, the optics of light, the effect on the human mind, the shading of lines and colors and so much more. Vast curiosity, imagination, and a drive to learn through experimentation and hyper-keen observation were his hallmark traits. It's rare that such traits combine with that of a creative and ambitious genius, and at a time in which discovery and learning was so valued by humanity. There are so many life lessons to be understood. But the ones that I'd like to draw on (note the pun) are his work on perspective, a favorite topic of mine, as well as shading.

First, shading. Mathematically, a line has no width and, hence, no volume. In nature, in everything we can see, we cannot see a line. We see a geometry, a volume, and, hence, in representing lines in our mind, we really see shading.

Leonardo experimented and worked to understand optics, light, and the volume and effect of shading. And we learn too. We are taught to think of the world as good and bad, right and wrong, and paths that are clearly defined. When, like in art and math, there are not lines without shades, paths are not as clearly delineated as our framing would like. It takes time and experience to understand that our greatest challenges and life-learning is when we are pushing boundaries of hard-drawn lines, and it is there that we find the shading.

Perspective, too, has a way of being fuzzy. As we look into the distance, items twice as far away are half the size, and so too we find that features blur, color is muted and faded. It is necessary to journey there to see clearly the features. It is necessary to keep in mind that as we look into our futures, those futures are never as clear as you may try to play them in your mind. They too have a lot of shading and blurring of features. It is wise to use perspective in life and planning, to see broad directions on where to go and why, but also to know that there are many things that cannot be seen clearly until you are there, and even then we find shading. Perspective gives us a point of view that, when used wisely, is invaluable, while shading reminds us of the complexity of life, keeping the world interesting, and challenging us always.

The Burden

Today will be a rainy day
I feel it in my bones
And in my bed, I'd rather stay

But I rise, creak and crack
The world expects it of me
So, put this burden on my back

Onto the day and into the rain
It is for me to carry on
No use or purpose to complain

The burden will never know
It just sits there and weighs
Heavy as it bends me low

I'll rest well when I'm dead
And the burden will fall gratefully
To another lucky someone instead

In the Smallness of Time

Pushed, turned, blown to there
Leaves and flotsam everywhere

Dreams and ambitions cast aside
Small in schemes of our mind's ride

Small moments of consequence
Of importance and preeminence

Magnifies the smallness of a time
Of a moment, of even this rhyme

Yet, small of many makes us complete
Beyond turbulence and troubles we meet

In smallness of time, a blink of a star
Be blessed in knowing...
In this moment, just who we are!

Time Traveled

Is it a moment when we close our eyes
Or is it years where memories play

Is time a measure or a summation
Of all we are and know

Is time traveled really a dream
And ghosts the echoes of our minds

Is our time here only and now
Or a summation of all we dream

Is our dreams and plans for future
Impelled by legacies past and present

Is it our condition to dream and wonder
Playing with memories we now own

Let time in all its glory always be our joy
In future, past and present in perfect harmony

Off to School

Off to school when first you know
It's beyond the home you really grow

A story has so many points of view
Every book and every chapter's new

Each year a story is added for you
Maybe crayon in finger paint when two

Soon pages turn ever faster
As life stories and plots we master

We build the stories that we live
Learning, loving, taking and we give

A chapter turns, and our story is clearer
Career, college and tests are nearer

No longer does someone read to you
You are responsible for your own point of view

Into the next chapter future burning
Pages written and more rapidly turning

Careers and life and loves are like blowing winds
Driving where and how the next chapter begins

Your children off to school, at various ages
You find consuming story as you help turn their pages

Before too long you are reading grandkids stories
Your book, their book, in chapters you revel in all their glories

So, it's back to school this time of year
So, write your grand story, bold, happy and without fear!

A walk on the beach on two different days: "By the Long Island Sound" and "The Next Day" show a difference in moods and the value of seeking that "next day" always in life….

By the Long Island Sound

Yesterday's sky was gloomy and gray
The ocean whipped by wind did spray

Birds treaded water in the sky
Screamed at the wind by and by

Walk was chilly, wind whipped my ears
Even my eyes bring some tears

Weather forcing some gloomy thought
Gray and foreboding ideas brought

Another soul on the beach, a photographer
Capturing birds on shore or floating in the air

At least it did seem someone else cared
For this morning and beach to be shared

Looking forward to vacation by the bay
Hope this works as a pleasant place to stay

Sure, it will clear up and happy we will be
For the next day, maybe brighter by the sea

The Next Day

*It's bright, it's beautiful and clear
Tide is up, waves sending up a cheer*

*It was desolate just yesterday
It is nearly crowded today*

*Step is lighter and mood bright
Everything seems suddenly right*

*A difference a day can make
A difference a mind can't shake*

*The foulest of gray thought of a day
The next day bright will wash it away*

*Loved ones in heart and mind
Fresh and bright with day aligned*

*A day like the next appreciated best
Like in life when compared with the rest*

*Let your every gray day end at night
There will be a next day shiny and bright*

Embracing Risks

I've written about how great and growing lives are driven by a relentless curiosity (see "Loving Curiosity" and "Of Perspective and Shading" and its value in how we navigate life.) True to "Thinking About It" and "Keep it Simple", I was thinking about the value of risk taking in one's life journey. I have expressed a philosophy that includes truthful self-evaluation, seeing the journey ahead of you from the vantage point of perspective, understanding that clarity is not possible, and that life and futures are always shaded. I encourage decision making based on perspective but also based on evaluations of options where the fewest assumptions are necessary to see successful outcome, and yet I'd be remiss if I didn't add the need for risk taking. Every day in life has inherent risks. We may be prudent. We may seek to avoid failure and danger, but it is ever present. Randomness and chance both play a role in our lives, in good ways and in bad. In a way, circumstances are a part of every life that we can either embrace—"Dancing with Circumstance"—or we can spend our days decrying to each other the consequences of circumstance. So, too, our decisions and our path always include options of relatively greater or lesser safety. I believe that if we are curious, and investigative, if we are able to see past the risk with perspective, if we keep it simple and think about it, then we can master too the risks of our lives and world. All interesting stories involve taking a risk. As my grandfather used to always say, "Take a chance, Columbus did." I'm sure he meant it in a fun and casual way, but I see those words differently in the passage of time. Quite possibly, it was his way of saying that in all life, in every game of cards or game of life, there are choices and risks. But there is no great story, there are no great wins, and no great loves without taking a risk. And when you do, do so with passion, and know very well that "Passion is a Dragon."

Passion

Passion may be the human trait that makes us most interesting. Passion is desire given a name. It's fear managed. It's what makes us love, it's what makes us excel in the arts, in business, and in sports. Some say that there is a fine line between genius and madness. I think that fine line is passion controlled versus passion uncontrolled. Contained by perspective, wisdom and improved on by practice, passion is what can make us great. Think about the athlete who excels at his or her sport … it's by passion that they excel. It is also at that border between perfection and destruction that we see passion play out and are fascinated to watch. A batter in baseball fails more than two-thirds of the time, yet he is great if he succeeds just that one third of time, because we know and understand the passion for their sport that they have conquered.

When we listen to a great musician, we know we are hearing passion. We want to not just listen, but we want to watch. We want to see how they are engulfed by their music and become that music, and they are always so close to the edge of madness. Think about why we pay hundreds to go to a concert when for a few bucks we can listen to a perfect rendition of their work in the convenience of home? Same with a dancer—how close they are to failing, yet they perform flawlessly because they've controlled a passion through practice and perspective. They know what they can do and what they cannot instinctively … and because they've been to the other side before. Passion uncontrolled can be destructive and consuming. Passion controlled is productive, wonderful and the greatest of all human traits.

I saw a dancer once, and it occurred to me how she was controlling passion, managing her dragon as it seemed to me—making passion productive. In our minds, our hearts and our souls, we struggle to find, control and manage our dragon. We must put ourselves in the proper and perfect state of mind to manage our passions—proper level of restraint and control with perspective and wisdom as we dance with our dragon.

Passion is a Dragon

Settle thoughts, settle heart, keep in line
Look to the future, remembering the past
Be in the present a perfect state of mind

Passion is a Red Dragon that must be named
Contained, controlled and yet wild just the same
Work on it, train it, the dragon must be tamed

Fire in my soul lets the dragon fly as needed at time
Dance with it, control and make it work, others see
But keep in the present a perfect state of mind

See the sunset beautiful and perfectly framed
Then settle, enjoy and let the dragon dream
Sky dark, moon and stars more than can be named

Deep at night, the dragon stirs in its sleep
Keeping it alive, listen to it influencing me
Productive, think, protecting me in my castle keep

See joy and laughter and love of friends
Be in the present a perfect state of mind
Comfort in soul that such beauty never ends

Dragon sleeps but still there to awaken in time
Events and time, emotions and rhymes
Be in the present always a perfect state of mind

Be Lucky

Over the course of some many poems, I've tried to convey some of what I feel is accumulative wisdom about life and thought that, if considered and followed, it should enhance the probability of finding success in life and business. I've pressed the need for perspective, of being curious, of being passionate and willing to take risks and of course the need for self-evaluation–to know your own capabilities and be honest about it and then to stretch and climb the mountains in front of you. Create a lifelong passion for learning and accomplishment.

What I've not yet talked about is "luck". I've written about life's lottery, which is a bit of luck in where you were born, what country your parents managed to get you to, and how the sacrifices of our ancestors brought you to a point in your life where you have opportunities for success.

Most people get some break in life, an opportunity that presents itself, in part out of luck ... Many will never have the perspective to see the opportunity; they will only see the problem. Some will be too timid to explore it, or if they do, will realistically lack the talent or passion to exploit it. However, getting that opportunity is something of a bit of chance, of luck, and we can increase prospects of this occurring by expanding our network, expanding our experiences, and being open to seeing change as a potential opportunity. Furthermore, be ready! Develop the wisdom and capability to respond to opportunity when it knocks ... and then work hard and be persistent. Climb that mountain! If you don't, you'll find that there are so many other talented people who are also out there looking for their chance as they go by you.

Be Lucky!
I know I have been!

About the Author

Mike Varga is an executive in the engineering services business with significant aerospace experience. He was a founder and CEO of a small business that was successfully acquired in early 2016.

Besides golf and occasional sailing, his hobby for the past few years has been providing his musings on a website for close friends and family. He has two daughters and four grandchildren. He lives with his wife, Yvonne, 11 miles from the Gulf of Mexico.